MW00654454

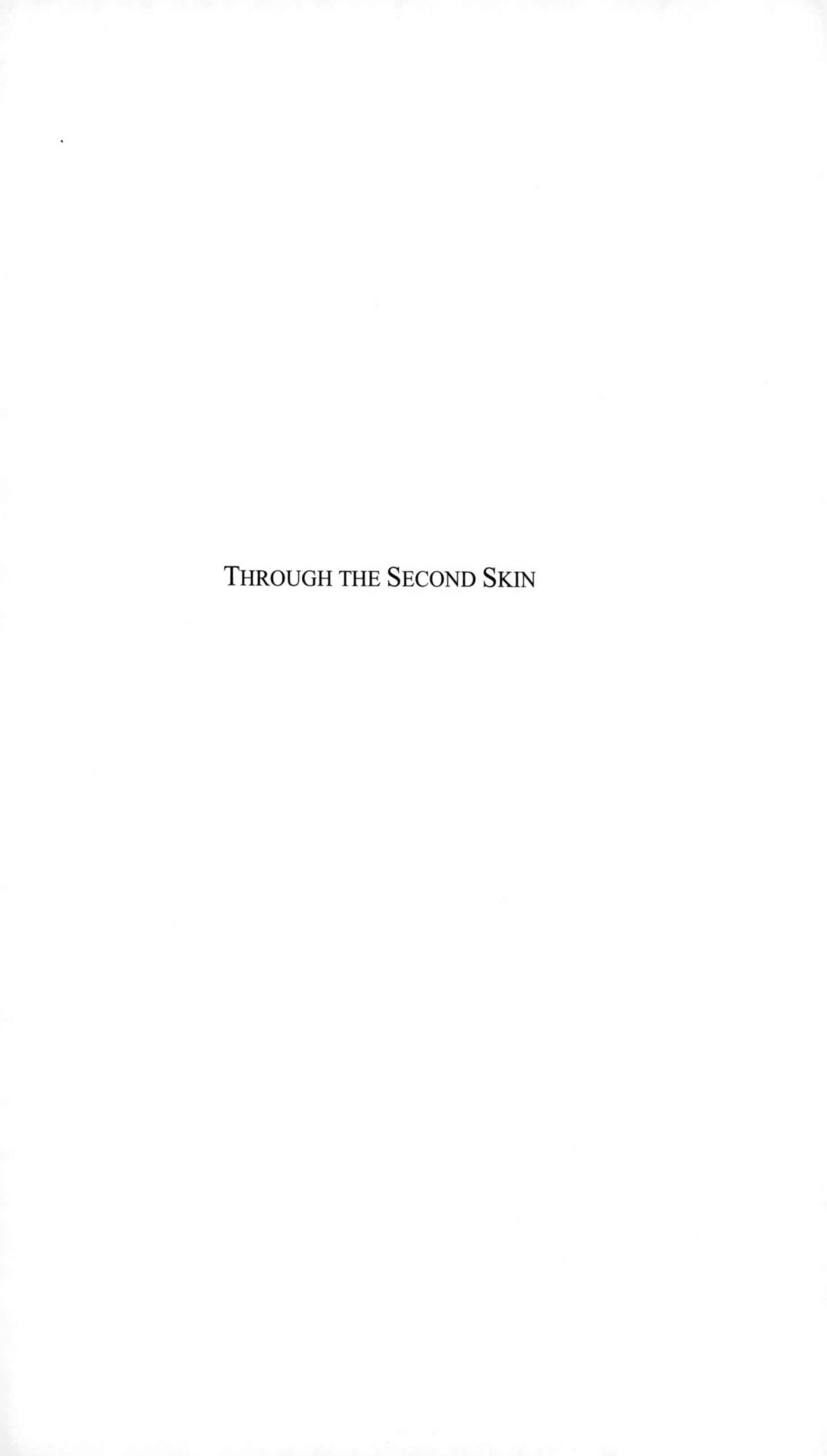

THROUGH THE SECOND SKIN

Through the Second

* *

SKIN

DEREK SHEFFIELD

* *

ORCHISES
WASHINGTON
2013

Library of Congress Cataloging-in-Publication Data

Sheffield, Derek.
Through the second skin / Derek Sheffield.
p. cm.
Poems.
ISBN 978-1-932535-28-0 (alk. paper)
I. Title.
PS3619.H45146T47 2013
811'.6—dc23
2012029297

*

Since this page cannot legibly accommodate them, credits and acknowledgments will be found on page 93.

*

ORCHISES PRESS
P. O. BOX 320533
ALEXANDRIA, VA 22320-4533

G 6 E 4 C 2 A

TABLE OF CONTENTS

---

*

*

for GABI, ZOEY, and KELSEA

*

And why should you come like sparrows for prayer crumbs,
Whose hands can dabble in the world's blood?

—R.S. THOMAS

Ornithology 101

Now that you have staked their skeletons,
eyed the scope of a throat, prodded
strutted white ribs, pinched
a wishbone for resilience, thumbed
a keeled sternum's edge still trying
to steer scattered feathers, stroked
a hummingbird's mum iridescence, ruffed
the white down of a great egret
slit and stuffed as last year's final project,
sprinted with a severed wing to catch
the physics, given new vision
to a blackbird with two dabs of cotton,
you can leave with an *A* in class *Aves*.
Now that you have looked through birds, you see
the diagrammatic movements of geese
across the blue sky, dotted lines
narrowing a million years. You expect
from every American goldfinch thistles
and sadness, and when you walk out
among the world's perches and Latinate streaks
at the edge of sight, the air is feathers
measuring the bones of your face.

A Good Fish

Jerk that bitch, urges my guide,
and I give my shuddering pole
a jerk, hooking the throat
of the first steelhead of my life.
Reel 'em, he mutters and revs the motor.
I horse my pole and reel and horse.
The boat's mascot whines, her claws
clicking. *Let it take some line.*
My father, uncle, and cousin
are reeling. *First fish!* they shout,
and I shout, *What a fighter!*
A silver spine touches the air.
There, he points, *a hen. And guess what?*
She's gonna join the club,
somehow spotting in that glimpse
the smooth place along her back
where a fin had been snipped.
He leans over the gunwale, dips a net,
and scoops her into the boat.
She is thick with a wide band
of fiery scales, slap-

slapping the aluminum bottom.
Welcome to the club, he says,
and clobbers her once, and again,
and once more before she goes still.
A bleeder, he says, shaking his head
and handing her to me. I curl
a finger through a gill the way
you're supposed to, determined
not to let her slip and flop
back to the river, a blunder
I'd never live down. A good fist.
Fish, I mean. A good fish.

To Do

You've planted and weeded and wheelbarrowed,
now tapping a pencil, trying to remember
the next thing—what was it?—when a shape
drops from the sky, shudders and stops
at a tree—red blotch—whack, whack.
A creature big enough on this slow spring day
to make you mutter, *Ho-*
meric, exactly like the popeyed codger
in the John Wayne flick when he sees
how the bride and groom have broken
their bed. A big, wild woodpecker. Imagine
how it would feel to glimpse, like this,
an ivory-billed, that one they say
(if that's what they saw) is the last,
epic of the air, boomerang to be
and not. But could it be
this one will make it for real?
Make it beyond lit screens,
this pileated inkling now hopping into brisk beats
of loopy flight. And now almost
in your grasp, the day's next thing,

when a rattled, rising shriek riddles the air.
Again. And again you're just beginning:
a nest of electric light, a boy
waiting for the bus and laughing
at the cartoon bird laughing like crazy.

HOLY TRAFFIC AT THE UNIVERSAL GATE

> A correct account of causality holds a special significance
> for Schopenhauer because he thinks philosophers use
> causality to smuggle God into the universe.
> —*The Giants of Philosophy*

One takes the Good that is handed to him
and wonders where to run, white hair spiking
Einsteinishly as he tucks the bundle
under his dark robe. Behind him, a line
of tireless postulators leads back
through the intersection of Eternity
and Moment, curves stoop-shouldered
around an axiological forest, and disappears
behind the Hill of Human Understanding.
Some pontificate with short stabs of their pipes
while others pass the time and the space
smoking, opening their mouths and blowing
O after dissipating *O:* no
matter, no air. The ones in front cannot help
but rub their beards and consider
going on the lam. As two hypergiants
of the border guard escort the first in line
to a cell of dark matter, the next

steps up for the frisk, looking now
as if he's expecting. "It's the Expanding Edge—"
he might say, patting his stomach.
Or he might say nothing, let nothing
do the work that nothing can.

As a Species Flies from Extinction, Consider the River

In passing clarity, curled
Feather and flash, see
The brown eyes
Of the world. What rocks
Are these? Fourteen million
Orbits refract this
Influence of spreading center, polarity
Spinning a water strider's legs like needles
To the pulse in every
Tongue. Below Skookumchuck, the shape
Of a bird's neck in sleep
Holds the current and the memory
Of ancient ice releasing
Mad gleaming, rivulet violence.
Could this etch of avian glyph
And fluxing flurry of onwardness
Bear the conception that ending
Is myth? The syllabics of scree, too,
Clatter before a buck's long skid
And purling swim, and the river
He rises from and shakes

From his antlers, the river
Of sunlit droplets
Pelts the rocky dust
Around his tracks.

Body Count

The bright weapons that sing in the atmosphere, ready to pulverize
the cities of the world, are the dreams of giants without a center.
Their mathematical evolutions are hieratic rites by Shamans without belief.

—Thomas Merton

They could not reach us.
They were nothing, silhouettes
we fired at. I got one, I said
to the ones on my side who could not stop
their rifles from drawing shot after
parallel shot, whose eyes shrank
to decimal points.

Then faces filled the shadows,
elliptic lines crossing ours.

In room after room, we lie.
From the half-light of one,
I listen for bedsprings and floorboards.
How many? I cannot stop
aiming for accuracy.

Formulaic: each lung sac

expands so many times per minute.
If I could only breathe
without breath, snuff the racket
beneath my skin, that blubbering
muscle making of my blood
zero after zero.

Living on James Wright

As they aim their laser pens
over charts, ornithologists calmly explain
the slow, sloping descent
of neotropical migrants.
They open factual arms in dim rooms
to show the size of Ohio—puckering widows
and one dirty river become the yardstick
for South America's clear-cuts.

If he were here, he would catch
the yellow warbler
that clutched my hand today, its
song of hurried sweets.
As he broke his lines for the warm
tap of its heart, a hobo
would appear, and a boy with rusty hair,
a real deadeye, sighting
down a secret barrel for one more
slurred silhouette.

Even the blips of northbound vireos
along the branch between Americas
would cast in his lyric a green wing.
I heard him once, a lone Ohioan
opening his throat

three thousand miles from the gathering
outlines of his state. And when
that yellow warbler lay
in my palm, thinned from its journey,
a breath of fierce light searching me
with one dark eye, I stood
as if I did not breathe
and only wind could move me.

Search Engine

Stooped over a desk, fingers
tapping, a man squints

as if he looks into the sun
instead of a screen. Beyond

his wall, branches stir
over a lengthening line, ants

on the crawl. With taps,
clicks, and whirrs, he ventures

wider. With shaken bodies,
bees tell the way

from nest to nectar. All day
he scans bright hits

as a night he didn't see coming
arrives like a dream

of mute talons descending.

Aubade

Waking, I find a still form,
a bird whose aim was to sweep
past our sleeping faces, to be
that glorious gust, or trumpet spurt

of dawn, and not this lidless eye
upturned below our window.
I kneel and slide my fingers
under fading warmth. A limp,

soft sparrow. Scaly talons
clutched as I carry it like an egg
beyond my yard and toss it
in brief revival back to the woods.

The knock did not wake my wife,
and neither do I, slipping into bed
to lie beside her with open eyes.
Light takes the hill, the trees,

our house into its definite grasp,
all the sparkling edges revealed,
and all I hear, all I want to hear,
is breath after breath.

The Accretions

> I understand that Blake would have us see heaven
> in a grain of sand, but some days nature must bow
> before the accretions of our fantastic species.
>
> —*from a friend's letter*

So that's what the sun has been up to
prostrating its shining before mine
as I savor the genius of knife and fork
with respect to steak. Every day ending
in a bow, a flattering reminder
to save room for that saffron custard

crème brûlée, that pinnacle
caramelized in Paris as nowhere else.
On the Boulevard of Champions,
bankers dab their lips with cloth napkins,
merci, as the moon lowers herself
before Pepsi and the pyramids,

vanishes entirely at the thought
of airplanes, alphabets, and baseball.
Van Gogh's *Wheatfield with Crows*
deserves a thumbs up. Or should we count

black birds flapping over golden stalks?
Had the postal service delivered your letter

early, say 1973,
and Mother helped me with *accretions*
and *species*, I would have reached for a bag
of Army men. Nothing slowed my breath
with such joy as aiming the bazooka man
in mud I made with spit

at the standing man, his rifle
butted to shoulder, right eye fixed
on the one lobbing a grenade—
a pattern pure as any stand of trees.
Father was yelling about the credit card,
a door was slamming, and I was kneeling in light

that had split the darkness
to reach my tongue and the sound of guns.
In a far land, men whose green minds
were not plastic were crawling
into the ground, making of their lives
black stems, red blossoms.

Prayer with Game

As far as you can see are seabirds
            that won't stop dying, won't stop
making a froth-slicked slag heap

of this beach, this riot of wings
            restless as rats. You can't help
but watch them peck and scrabble

across sand and rock, every species
            beyond the reach of wave
after wave shushing in—and that anemic C

of moon that looks to be floating
            just above their flocked panic.
Bloom is no name for *this*, these splashes

of red feathers, of loons lying
            in white collars like clergy
fresh from a stabbing. They won't stop

crying, shrill infants left to the elements,
cry after rising cry
until you pray for joystick and screen,

a chance to plug in and propel
your radiant self beyond this level.
Instead of phytoplankton, gigabytes

and a fair fight in which you could bring it,
breeze over waves and click
each ruby icon of each loon eye and win.

The Ramp

I.

Slowly rolling a steel wheelchair, rubber vein
bulging under the skin of his left arm,
he watches. Neil hammers, Travis saws, I measure,

and nothing, we know, squares in his sight,
carpenter, grandfather, overseer.
On the weekly drive to church, our fathers

swerved as they pointed to the houses
he built, reciting the names of owners
long moved on or dead.

He'd work all day and come home in a shirt
still holding its creases. One last shim
and we stand in the sawdust of our sins,

watching him steer down our skewed cuts.
A bit steep, but it will do
for Sabbath and dialysis.

II.

Neil swings a sledge, Travis stacks the scrap, and I jerk
my hammer in reverse, cleats jangling to concrete.
From the doorsill, no one reckons our mistakes.

Wood wrenches free of wood, and I hear again
how he wanted to see *all* his grandchildren
again. In the two weeks it took for his blood

to poison him, he wanted to see me
immersed in water lit by stained glass.
We sweep, straighten, and lock the house.

Anyone watching would see
three young men in jeans and T-shirts
walking back to their truck. He would see

the one in the middle pause
for something on the ground,
a bent nail, say, to hold and to keep.

Delicious Apocalypse

When I imagine it now, I'm no
longer thirteen and revving across the
charred earth on my motorcycle, searching for
other survivors who say, What would we do without
you and your Suzuki DS 100? Now, like you and everyone,
I'm gone. The trees and sunlight, crickets and rivers going on
without us. Stop signs and birds. No more toilets clogged.
I would miss my friends as much
as anything, like the one beside me.
He's my father's age, squinting over a white beard.
We are digging through the cab
of his pickup, Red, a little diesel
you have to treat right, especially in winter. When we find
enough pennies, he hands them to the girl at the counter
along with two dollar bills. A fair trade we believe the
same day once a week, this day we give ourselves to
unwrap greasy mushroom burgers and chew
one bite at a time, this hour dividing
our work and ending with each
shining finger licked.

Breathing in Wartime

Glass magnifies two bulging pupils:
a goldfish peers beyond its bowl,
perhaps as far as the windows

of the next building
where a man in dress shirt and tie
appears, gathers papers from a desk, disappears.

The fish makes o's with thin, gold lips,
stubborn little o's I mimic,
opening and closing my mouth.
Repeatedly reflected in the windows

where the desk remains vacant, a jet
ripples, shrinks and stretches,
tail fin catching the light,
the spikes of a silent explosion.

*

…see how the brook
In that white wave runs counter to itself.
It is from that in water we were from.

—ROBERT FROST

From a Cabin in the Hardwoods

Whatever you do, don't tell Gabi
about the four wood roaches. Every fall
she shouts, "Where do they come from?"
her eyes spying yet another
leaf-legged bug perched on the railing
where her hand almost
landed. She doesn't hear
the chai tea dribbling into milk
as conversation, doesn't want to see
expression in the brittle gloss
of a carapace. There is no question
we live by relations. And so I write
through these pressed and dried fibers
to you. With you, I share the mystery
of the roaches who wandered in
from their floor of leaf rot, the two
who turned up slipping down the white
porcelain of the sink, one crouched
in the coffee filters, and one on the radio
waving thin antennae at my open hand,
asking only for your silence.

Firefighters Walk into Mountain Sports

Straight from flames, faces soot-slapped
and yellow jackets swishing,
they track cinders of century-wide pines
wrenched from root-sockets
and sucked skyward like bungled fireworks.
Blazes in their ears, they shout across aisles
and racks, thumbs hooked over belts
with curious assurance: whether they hold
Pulaski and shovel, or Polartec and Nike, the end
will come nameless, wearing the same face.

One models a hat, and they hoot.
If they wanted, they could howl
at such prices or the well-tanned skier
in search of a deal and a fit,
clomping seven times across the store
and back in orange Atomics.

Slim and pig-tailed, the girl
who rips their receipts from the register
is the last line they walk

before flinging again comets of earth
at something like the sun unhinged.
From their radio, a staticky voice,
the green world going black.

A Revised Account of the West

They never rode into any sunsets,
didn't slowly melt themselves
like witches into puddles,
or burst, man and horse fused
in one fell buck, one myth of ash
gone to the sinking mound.

They rode away from the doors
of saloons that opened to a twisting
dance of rock and sand:
no bright tunes played
and no feather boa
slid from a slender neck.

They rode instead toward
gaseous fusion, in the direction of
the photosphere as their shadows
pointed the way back
to town and a pair of boots
aimed crosswise in the dust.

Fuel

Dihedral shadows of plunging raptors
or sheer mammalian desire
drove the mice from dust to rubber,
pioneering up and over the Bridgestone,
a many-tailed whisper smuggled
between alternator and distributor, slipped
wire-like through greasy darkness.

Insulation scratched from every corner,
they swaddled themselves and began
to multiply, nipples pulsing
like nubby pistons, pink-skinned pups
suckling and sleeping—awake at a click
and rattled roar, every corner lit
by the sprung leaks of eye-gleams.

They build where they will and live
between the shades. No wonder
of a day's spin in their nosy twitches,
no worry of the one who bought this

container of contained explosion, the one
at the wheel whose first notion
of them will come when it won’t go.

Thinking up a New Power

Unlike oil, the wind is always there, sometimes.

—Frank Murkowski, former governor of Alaska

Sometimes there and others
there. Again it slides through, moves
over swaying stalks of kelp
or Anchorage with ease and all ways
sounding the same in Arabic

as English, Simoom
and Chinook. Clear monument
of moments gathered, it's here
when on its way: red flags flare,
headlines flip in the street,

and every far peak
blurs while buoyant seeds
float its democratic shoulders.
Birds know how to cup
its slight adjustments. Could its breath

be the way we breathe,
shifting, failing and strong? It is
our only state, offering
from the start an ocean depth
and the slightest nod.

Called by Winter

There's getting to be quite a throng down there.
Since the sexton took the job, he has seen his town,
his neighbors, his father lie slowly down.
Now he lowers his glasses to read
his map of the dead. Melvin Tucker today
whose Mary still dabs her face with rouge,
who teased the neighbor kid every snowfall,
"Did you order this?" The sexton remembers
his shy and smiling "no" as he peels unwieldy strips
of sod, baring the silence before he fires
the backhoe and makes it hunch and jerk its bent arm
and scoop bucket by darkening bucket.
Dirt heaps like a sleeper as he raises the pale,
partial resurrection of one bone
where it should not be, uncharted, unstoned,
and lowers it back to its echoing way.
He does not wonder who. Head deep
in the fresh gape, he squares by hand,
his breath fogging three feet from Miss Jackson.
Only once has he had to vault from caving earth.
A man of figures, he knows his work is not

bad luck, every plot over the years keeping
some track of him. He does it for a living, nodding
every visit to the carved letters of his father's name.
And after the mourners have gathered
and gone, in the deepest season he knows, he begins
with the lowering sun to fill the newly vacant
and roll the green lid back, again.

Song of the Lark

Barefoot among brown furrows, face lifted,
a girl has stopped, mid-step,
the sickle in her hand glinting
a question mark of light.

Beyond her, distance softens wheat stacks,
a house, trees, and half a world farther,
half the sun about to flare or flicker,
the saffron sky to blue or vanish.

If her brand of work has ever dulled the arc
of your body, if you've caught yourself
thinking this might be it—
pricks of stubble, insect buzz, and grit—

you would know there is no question
of time, that dawn is a word for dusk.
The single hesitation in this Old World
oil on canvas lies in her parted mouth

and eyes searching for what must be
a skylark perched, in Breton's best stroke,
beyond the frame, and warbling
without a smudge of weariness.

ALICE

Couch,
lamp,
teakettle,
picture—
Alice reclaims her words,
scrawls each on a paper scrap
and sticks it,
counter,
in the middle
of the white kitchen counter.
She was scrubbing dishes last Sabbath
when her pulse began to shudder
seventy years from her brain.
She snips, writes, and tapes
table,
chair,
clock.
We press our thumbs into the blue tracery
of her skinny wrist and count
the beats of a sparrow's wings.
Charlie adds wood to the stove

and tells her to leave her hands alone,
forget about the tea, sit down.
He opens a drawer to the fire opal
he will have set for this woman
he met fifty years ago
under an apple tree in Millersburg.
Seed-small in the middle
of his palm, the stone scintillates.
We check our count with a machine,
peeling the Velcro, the rubber slack
around Alice's arm, and do not know
what to trust. Alice writes
Bible.
Charlie stirs the coals.
We speak of weather, and Alice,
predicting wind and—
searches for the word she knows is there
like a misplaced butter dish.
She looks to the floor,
floor,
and says, *That*
thing,
thing,

thing,
shaking her hands, standing,
and this woman who believes
living is needle and broom, garden
and jar, who's been living
all her life, stops herself
at a word from Charlie, sits
and takes a breath.
We leave the machine listening
to the flutter inside her.
Charlie shakes our hands.
As we walk out the door, we see
a last paper sunlit in the window—
apple tree.

ANOTHER WORD

Long before I saw one,
  I heard a loon
    in my cousin's hands
cupped to his lips—willow.
  He tried to teach me how
    flesh could find that shape.
I hoped and hoped
  into a mouthpiece of thumbs
    but the air was empty.
Through this morning's rain,
  a loon tosses its call
    as if it were nothing,
and the sound, now,
  another word
    for far.

Anonymous Hawk

My friend mouths the names
of birds invisible
to him, and waxwing
becomes a lit candle, a shrink,
a fiery bottle. A veery turns
into a supplicant gouging his knees
on sacred stone, a poem.
Maybe a thousand names
will extinguish the shades
roosting in the corners
of his eyes. Perhaps
the cracked corn he scatters
faithfully into darkness
will call something whole.
Golden kernels spray
from his fist, pattering the dust
like shot. Not far
from where his face shadows
a window, softly calling,
I am not here,
in a patch of rattled thistles,

some kind of hawk draws
the instrument of its beak
down anonymous feathers
and the ground swallows the song.

Prayer with Fur

Down a scarp of gray rock and dust,
  not a brook, not even
    a rill, but a lick
dribbles, through sheer heat,
  all day and under every flood
    night sends. Mud the color of dusk
remembers an earlier slither,
  and skinned roots claw
    a coolness in air

flowing past my shins. I kneel
  and call Ginger to the water
    in my hands, a cold shock,
a splash of the first night
  out of the Garden,
    two people on their backs
under the unlocked stars,
  touching along arms and legs,
    silenced by a glittering distance.

Here, on the trail to Temple Ridge,
    my dog lowers her face, looks to mine,
      and laps, and keeps lapping
until my hands are open and empty
    but for stroke after stroke
      of her insistent tongue.

How We Look

Fur-fat and stock-still in the trail
	they appear to be looking
		into a mythic sky, posed
for a feral portrait, or a wish
	to draw us closer before they turn
		and level a frontal marmot scrutiny.
The way their noses aim askance
	says they're not here. Or we
		are gone. Or we are here

but they're not sure.
	Upright on boulders, they are ready
		to tumble at the shrill signal
if we become, in a blink,
	by sneeze or shuffle, believable.
		Our pack-heavy shapes, gathered
in their sky, look up
	to Shuksan: how distant

and present it juts, how sharp
a lookout, clarity
we envy through tilted glass
until from every nowhere
the whiteout. When the peak
disappears, we turn and labor
down the moraine, switch-
backing like mules silently spaced
in the falling snow.

While we drive our miles
and climb to bright rooms, they settle
below in a general huddle,
slowing for their long dream.
Between one flake
and the infinite next, one pulse beat
and the second, our burdened forms
waver and loom, weave and are gone.

As Seen Through a River

The bank of silt cools
            my bare skin where I kneel
and pore over a skittish mob
            of water striders whose spidery,

wire-thin limbs do not
            pierce and sink, but press
into being supple dimples,
            and as they stir they talk

in clear syllables, a jittery council
            I can only watch. Around us,
sagebrush flares from hills of hot dust,
            a hundred years of the tribe

of green flames. Power lines rise and dip,
            buzz out of sight. I must say something
terrible as I reach in, for my bugs
            twitch away in rippled

exclamation, my pale arm dangling
        and my face from the underside—
a wobbly thing in the middle
        of ring after booming ring.

Oystermen

What comfort to see them trudge on the tideland
back and forth with nets and buckets,
dredging for puddles of ripened, lung-shaped oysters.
Bundles of thick coats and boots, they plant lanterns
and hunker in small glows to pick
secret after knobby, clicking secret.

Lowest tides draw them late night down
the bank of surf grass, crunching across sand dollars
and crab shells, clattering from the rocks
and slurching to their muddy bed while I slip
into mine. With slowing eyes, I watch them roam
and dazzle like prehistoric fireflies,

call out over the blue-green mussel worm
that twists a slimed gleam in the muck,
the severed arm of the six-rayed star,
some kind of eye globbed on a stick. The one
with the roughest hands keeps to himself
until a dying fire coaxes him open for the children.

I wake before dawn and they are there,
gathered breath steaming as they spangle
the wet emptiness and clump in mud-heavied boots.
At every bright lamp shucked
out of the dark by a joggled lantern,

I want to surge down and labor shoulder
to shoulder, grab the ridged, slippery shells
in my pale hands, break each gritty fruit
from its cluster and become something other
than their midden ghosting the shore,
the relinquishing moon of jellyfish—to do
a work of weight, of being
one of the shades among the lights
before the cold sea climbs my legs.

Between Highway 2 and the Wenatchee

Splashes pulled me over and down
to the sand. What looked from the car
like boiling in the river was a collective shudder,
thrash of fin and sporadic scale.

With a clatter of rocks, a couple
clad in camouflage appears. "Fall run," I say.
He nods and glasses a wet smack
where one buck drives off another.
"Men!" she says and winks.
He wears a cowboy hat over a dark moustache.
Her curves press against her landscape,
cleavage in a V of leaf shapes. "Anadromous,"
I say, for the mere feel of the word
for breathing two worlds. Another hen
lashes herself against the gravel.

Bear tracks led them here. "You can get two a year,"
he says, "one for each side of the mountains."
They're here for their second.
"Seen any?"

And a black bear emerges
again from the brush behind my house,
flaring her long ears and crinkling her snout
during slow seconds
while two cubs, with clumsy shuffles
through stems and leaves, appear.
My wife holds our daughter
as I offer the soft growl of a new word.
The mother's fur nearly blond,
the cubs swinging dark heads, snuffing.

"Sorry," I say, shaking my head.
She says, "You can use anything,
black powder, a bow—you can even shoot the cubs
but nobody does."

"Still enough light to bag a bear,"
he says, and they turn
and walk back to the road

as I turn back to the river
and the bears watching us watch them.

*

Pebbles cannot be tamed
to the end they will look at us
with a calm and very clear eye

—ZBIGNIEW HERBERT

shrinking man who battled
the spider for cake crumbles, wielding only a needle
in that never-ending basement night? No starlight
as the story ended sobbingly for his wife and her
lake-sized tears splatting while mine sneaked
between mouthfuls of popcorn. He grew
tiny enough to step, finally, through
a square of wire screen, venturing
into a morning where the sun
flamed like a million suns,
a midge roaring overhead.
Our last sight: a staunch
minuscule walk
toward a grass-
bladed, beetle-
fraught
jungle.
The sequel
is particle physics
confiding our hero

made it: the big kid
on the molecular block,
at home in a world of excited
atoms. Sir Galileo slurps a cola
descrying inertia, and Whitman
flings his wide hat from the back row,
a new poem coalescing in his transcendental
happiness for our diminutive explorer leading
a line's life that is really uncountable infinity, really
a trail of dots . . . and he is one, traveling on like a ray
from that unfinished morning, the reel of film, like anyone
we lose from this life, matching, exactly, the pace of our grief.

LUCKY

When Bradley laughed because Dean didn't even know
his rabbit's foot was cut from a real rabbit, Dean's thumb
froze mid-stroke, feeling a claw under the green fur.
No wonder he lost his popgun. No wonder
Laura beat him in the UNICEF drive. He counted
on his fingers all the things taken from him.

In the parking lot alive with children and parents
waving from car windows, he found bus six
and kept thinking about the foot in his pocket,
the prints it must have made along a river
or leading from a dark burrow.

When the bus stopped in front of his house,
he walked straight to the backyard
and chose a spot under the plum tree.
With his father's shovel, he dug a hole,
then placed the foot inside and covered it.
He knew it might take hours for the rabbit
to grow back. He waited on the porch.

If he sat there long enough, he thought,
he would see his mother's car.

Nest Site

—Mount St. Helens, Willow Flycatcher

Below her steaming dome,
a nest of dead stems

cups two hatchlings, blind wobblers
among bits of shell. Even the way

their willow sways above trickles
of snowmelt cannot make them

less unlikely, scruffy lumplings
slated to unlock their flight and stitch

this air of ours, this gray land
scorched into being. If there is an aim

to their snaps and sallies, their kind
of fletched breath, look for it

in skin-shut eyes flushed with life,
in the way a child keeps from sleep

as long as she can, cupping a flashlight
for the bloody glow of her hand.

Glass

Every night it happens
that insects converge on the lights they see,

see, see. In one lamp suspended
over a table, the galaxy

of need. Chasing thin rays
through darkness,

they drone, flutter, and smack
into something smooth, something

that turns them
into ticks under the clinks

of utensils, of us chewing the fat.
Always outside trying to get in

our swept caves with their poky limbs—
like all the birds whose beaks

snap wide in surprise
at the clear divide. It's a story

when it breaks:
a sharp-shinned plunging

after a finch, or what happened in Alaska
when antlers appeared

as if encased, then framed
in shattering, then a dun shock of fur

skidding across carpet. In the photo,
you can see the flash

in the shards, the daughter
reaching toward a dark eye.

On Turning One

A rumpled balance of bottom and belly,
my daughter stands—
and squeals as she shakes a sheet of wrapping paper
with one hand and everything she's got,
the way a father shakes a pen
before he tries again to sign his name.
Earth has hauled its blue
back to the space of her beginning,
and once again, she's a wobbling show
who sits heavily, teaching gravity
a lesson. She looks up—no,
we are not slipping through her hands
like yesterday's balloon
dwindling to a little sperm
against the sky. We are

exactly where she keeps us
whirling. One year ago she lay
on a metal scale, in air
empty of body, crying her first cries.
The nurse said it was a good thing, the louder

the better, as I kept my hands from reaching
toward shivering fists, shut eyes, and skin
pale as a mist out of nowhere.

She raises an arm and squawks.
More paper? Ribbons? We add keys
and wallet as she starts to wail. Nothing
till a blur at the edge of sight, a zip
of iridescent pinprick
framed in the window, sipping sugar water.
She follows our gaze, growing quiet.
This we are certain of, this hummingbird
and its need for sweetness. Light
is what makes the red around its throat
shimmer, and we know, too,
the name for this place is *gorget*,
which sounds like *gorgeous*.

Near Wild Grasses

An afternoon like a loose grasp, a second skin
  of breeze and blue, just right
    for a stroll, and a snake sliding along
happens, by chance of scent or heat, to turn
  into a yard where a girl is making
    her pigtails wiggle, chatting
with the doll in her hands, returning its smile
  with hers. She does not notice me
    watching from the road
as a lipless mouth and eyes
  like insect eggs, glassy fractures,
    draw closer. Odds are
this notorious pattern of blotches
  will bruise no one. The tail's golden hive
will not rouse. This rattler
  will almost certainly stay
    secret, pulling its belly length
by length away through weeds
  and wilder grasses. The girl will go on
    shaping the sand of her sandbox
into a place where her doll can live.

And I will resume my walk,
struck only by the intimation
of earth's unruly beauty. But I go
to the door, knock, and say,
Just to let you know,
and the mother asks the favor,
looking to her daughter.
As I hesitate, consider, and reconsider,
over strides her neighbor, Heinz,
an old German, a grandfather
who says, *Oh ya, it's a big one,*
takes the shovel the mother brings
and barks, *Stand back.* The rattler
licks at the air with a tongue
flimsy as a creeper's tendril.
Gripping the shovel with both hands,
he lunges and pins the head,
bearing down, and the rattler writhes
like boiled water, like leaves
in a thrashing gust. A crunch
as the blade pushes through, coils
unwinding, still. The mother
wants to see it dangling

like a half-filled inner tube
  before he carries it, head
    and body, into the brush.
Thanking me, the mother
  holds her daughter, who stands
    quietly, watching me
walk down their drive to the road
  that takes me past other yards.
    At the house with green doors,
I am home. My daughter squeals
  where she sits on the floor.
    As I bend to lift her into my arms,
she grabs my cheeks and sticks out
  her tongue, wanting to know this man
    who is becoming her father.

The World's Other Side

In Japan, when you die, they wheel
what's left of you out of the incinerator,
and what's left of your family takes turns
picking with special chopsticks.
It looks like they have gathered to dine
over a dead campfire, but they are not,
of course, eating you. They are feeding you
to the round mouth of an urn:
only in pieces, Father, to the fire.
In their bright swimsuits,
my daughters spill warm sand over my skin
as I lie still, watching the sun
needle the sky. The baby licks her fingers
to tell, perhaps, if I am ready, her bald head
white with lotion, her mouth full
of vowels. The older one says nothing
above the ocean's slow rush,
but scoops and pats to get me done
and gone. I've never been to Japan,
but once, a globe of glass
found me at the clear end of a wave.
It drifted from the other side, Mother said.
Cold and slick, it glistened as I held it up
with both hands and looked through
to the green flames of the sun
before tasting the salt with my tongue.

Bye-bye

The animal of winter is dying,
its white body everywhere
in collapse and stabbed at
by straws of light, a leaving
to believe in as the air
slowly fills with darkness
and water drains from the tub
where my daughter, watching it
lower around her, feeling it
go, says about the only thing
she can as if it were a long-
kept breath going with her
blessing of dribble and fleck.
Down it swirls a living drill
vanishing toward a land
where tomorrow already
fixes its bright eye on a man
muttering his way into a crowd,
saying about the only thing
he can before his body
goes *boom*. And tomorrow,

I will count more dark shapes
tumbling from the sky, birds
returning to scarcity, offering
in their see-sawing songs
a kind of liquidity.

The One We're Spiraling Into

When Mount St. Helens blew
        that May day in the last millennium,
my father steered us through ash falling like snow,
        wipers ticking past another empty car.
Where did they go? And here I am,

        driving a mute blast of sunlight
with friends, asphalt and what's left
        of the woods, something like flagpoles
bristling on something like Ground Zero
        even as we begin to see

a gritty soil. Where smoke once curled
        from chimneys, a glistening rain
of spiders led to lark and elk, swallow
        and salamander. No more cabins
or dinner bells, but so much lupine

        you'd swear volcanoes exult in violet.
Even this pumice crunching under every step
        won't sink. *So much life,*

we say, hiking back to the car. Cheryl hopes
for a Dairy Queen, and Simmons clicks

through a thousand photos as we coast
the curves toward sea level, tired bodies
swaying together in time. Across the lake
to our left, a thousand trunks
still float like sticks in a game.

Then the future comes up, the one
we're spiraling into, and JP says,
Sure as shit wouldn't bring kids into this
world, in a way that chills my groin.
And Elizabeth observes, a stone

in her lap the size of a skull,
This is young enough to be my child.

Getting It Done

for Charles Wilson, M.D.

Naked below the waist and on your back,
you shake your doctor's hand. "Call me Chick,"
he says, snapping on a pair of gloves.
You've never heard that one, but you'd rather
a Chick did what this man is about to do
than your logger neighbor, Chuck.
You've driven two mountain passes to get to Seattle
and this specialist's reputed pianist's touch,
and you can't see him knobbing a skidder
through the stumps of a clear-cut. GET 'ER DONE
is not bumper-stuck to the rear of his Prius. No,
you're certain as you lie with your legs open
you've found a woodsman of another kind
whose fingertips have butterfly kissed the keys
of countless men and counting, little Amadeuses
that just now adjust a gooseneck lamp,
deftly tape your shaft to your belly, and begin
to swab your scrotum. Your eyes fix
upon the photo deliberately hung for all the men
who have lain here and all the Richards to come.

(Do his nights swim with lampreys, condoms
riddling every slosh and slither, salt
returned to salt in blind migrations of the ribbed
and the tipped?) It's a family in what looks to be a park
and—and an "Ohhh" escapes your mouth as if
you're about to sing, *Say can you,*
as Chick digs for a vas like a granny after a weed.
One hand pinches a clamp on every furtive strip
of your hog soul, while the other pelts your left
testicle with lidocaine. The mother and daughter
watch as the father tosses the son into the air,
arms upraised in a skewed U, their smiles
framed in bright swarms of autumn leaves.
Chick, too, is smiling as he hands you
a pocketknife that bears his clinic's name.
And you're up and walking like a man with an egg
on a spoon, mincing past the receptionist
who nods as if *Come again* is about to slip
from her lips. A pale man in the waiting room
watches your every step to the glass door
and out into the rinsed air of April, a breath
of fluttery forms and teetering songs,
and stems everywhere about to bloom.

FINISHING TOUCHES

for Chelcee Miller

Then it was morning,
and together they went

up the wooden stairs
to her room. Bed,

dresser. Pens left out
across the table, paper

and scissors. All as they
knew it would be. All

but the window, where,
side by side and whole,

her handprints.
They crossed the room

(she must have stood on a chair)
and moved their faces close

to whorls of fingertip
and palm: skeletal, deliberate

as concrete. And began to see
houses across the valley

where other children
were opening their eyes

and a long, gray river
steaming in the sun.

Sometimes I Risk

our lives, driving her   to school, tilting
the mirror   till the road
behind gives way   to the one
in her face   till I nearly
steer by the reflection   of her
reflection: chewing mouth,
eyes that flick   from thing
to each (through her)   momentous
thing. “What house   is *that*?” as we pass
a winery, eyebrows   leaping, dimples
dimpling. My see-   through highway,
revealing at once   what passes without
passes within,   a secret
I must keep, for if   she sees
me seeing me   in her, my eyes
and dimples,   then we
are lost in her   self-consciousness.
I must be   an afterthought
to sip at the lip   of her streaming
immediacy, for   my eyes
to oscillate   between the broken

yellow line
in her bangs and teeth,
and reckless glass
at what

and gaps
road ahead
aimed back
will go on

Darwin's Eyes

He kept seeing himself, a swallow
peeking from its nest, moss, the crawl
of a wasp across his study window.

And he kept having to drop everything and duck
as certain callers appeared in the mirror
he'd aimed at the front door.

A beak he could understand. A talon
was a hand holding his own. It was the eye,
with its vicious complexity, that stabbed at him—

lightning bolts of doubt,
a cyclopean stare, ten years his *Origin*
stewing in a stack of notes.

And the eye, perhaps, why he went back,
after all was said and begun,
to the worms, spending his last years

watching them as his fingers
wriggled over piano keys, exploring up
the scales and down, concerto

and dirge. His first passion, his final,
those tender needles with their dark impulse
to feel all around them our earth.

Acknowledgments

I am grateful to the editors of the following publications, where the poems in this book, sometimes in different form, first appeared:

Alaska Quarterly Review: "The One We're Spiraling Into"
Crab Creek Review: "Alice," "Anonymous Hawk," "Fuel," "How We Look"
Ecotone: "Darwin's Eyes," "Living on James Wright"
Floating Bridge Review: "From a Cabin in the Hardwoods"
The Georgia Review: "The Accretions"
Hampden-Sydney Poetry Review: "Between Highway 2 and the Wenatchee"
Hayden's Ferry Review: "Another Word"
In Posse Review: "Prayer with Fur"
The LBJ: Literary Arts, Avian Life: "Aubade"
Lyric Poetry Review: "Glass"
Margie: The American Journal of Poetry: "Near Wild Grasses"
Nimrod: "Song of the Lark"
The North American Review: "Ornithology 101," "Breathing in Wartime," "Body Count"
Orion: "On Turning One," "Delicious Apocalypse"
Passages North: "Living on James Wright"
Poet Lore: "Remember the Incredible," "The Ramp," "Holy Traffic at the Universal Gate," "Firefighters Walk into Mountain Sports," "Thinking up a New Power," "As Seen Through a River"
Poetry: "A Good Fish," "To Do," "*Bye-bye*," "The World's Other Side"
Poetry Northwest: "Oystermen"
Pontoon: Anthology of Washington State Poets (Floating Bridge): "Lucky"
River of Memory: The Everlasting Columbia (University of Washington): "As a Species Flies from Extinction, Consider the River"
Salt River Review: "A Revised Account of the West"
The Southern Review: "Finishing Touches," "Getting It Done"
Wilderness: "Nest Site"

I am also indebted to the editors of these anthologies where the following poems were published:

A Sense of Place: The Washington State Geospatial Poetry Anthology: "How We Look"
Ecopoetry: A Contemporary American Anthology (Trinity): "Darwin's Eyes," "A Good Fish"
Family Matters: Poems of Our Families (Bottom Dog): "The Ramp"
Limbs of the Pine, Peaks of the Range: 26 Northwest Poets (Rose Alley): "Ornithology 101," "The Ramp," "Remember the Incredible, "Firefighters Walk into Mountain Sports"
Many Trails to the Summit: Poems by 42 Northwest Poets (Rose Alley): "Near Wild Grasses," "Song of the Lark," "How We Look," "As a Species Flies from Extinction, Consider the River," "Darwin's Eyes," "Breathing in Wartime"
New Poets of the American West (Many Voices): "A Good Fish"
Poem, Revised (Marion Street): "Ornithology 101"
Terrain.org: "As a Species Flies from Extinction, Consider the River"

Some of these poems also were included in two chapbooks: *A Revised Account of the West* (2008), which won the inaugural Hazel Lipa Environmental Chapbook Award judged by Debra Marquart (*Flyway*/Iowa State University), and *A Mouthpiece of Thumbs* (Blue Begonia, 2000).

"Ornithology 101" won the James Hearst Poetry Prize, judged by Li-Young Lee, and "Aubade" was awarded the Sparrow Prize in Poetry.

"On Turning One" was awarded the Summer Solstice Broadside Contest and published as a letterpress broadside by Dwell Press. "Ornithology 101" was published as a letterpress broadside by Peasandcues Press.

"The Accretions" is for Jean-Paul Pecqueur.
"Anonymous Hawk" is for Gerald Tiffany.
"Another Word" is for Neil Sheffield.
"Called by Winter" is for Jack Johnson.
"From a Cabin in the Hardwoods" is for Allen Braden.
"Fuel" is for John Seaton.
"Ornithology 101" is for Dan Stephens.

"Remember the Incredible" is for Jan Wallace.
"The World's Other Side" is for Junko Bailey.

I would like to express my gratitude to Wenatchee Valley College for a sabbatical which allowed me to work on these poems. Also, the fellowships and residencies provided by Artist Trust, the Bernheim Arboretum & Research Forest, the Spring Creek Project, the Mount St. Helens Institute, the National Park Service, and Centrum were of enormous assistance.

I owe deep thanks to the people who read some or all of these poems at various stages and offered me their critical appraisal: Elizabeth Aoki, Allen Braden, Simmons Buntin, Catherine Coan, Andrew Gottlieb, Joseph Green, Dennis Held, Tim Houghton, Jack Johnson, Kevin Miller, Leslie Adrienne Miller, Jean-Paul Pecqueur, and Gerald Tiffany.

For the teachers, students, and friends that poetry has given me, I am grateful.

Thank you to my wife and daughters, my parents, and my sisters for their love and support.

And thanks to Roger Lathbury for giving these poems such a fine home.